SARK SAYINGS

MARI C. JONES &
MARTIN NEUDÖRFL

ILLUSTRATED BY MARTIN REMPHRY

BLLU
ORMÉ

Published by Blue Ormer Publishing
www.blueormer.gg

© Mari C. Jones & Martin Neudörfl 2022.
Illustrations © Martin Remphry 2022.
Reprinted 2023.

ISBN 978-1-8381076-9-7

INTRODUCTION

This book presents a collection of selected sayings and proverbs in Sark's native language, Sercquiais (*sehr-kh'oye*) (also spelt Sércê). Like the languages of Guernsey (Guernésiais) and Jersey (Jèrriais), Sercquiais is a Norman tongue. It is descended from Latin, brought by the Romans in the first century BC to the region which, several hundred years later, would be settled by the Norsemen and given the name Normandy.

In 933, the Channel Islands became annexed to the Duchy of Normandy, which itself was formally linked with England in 1066 when the seventh duke, William, became king of England by right of conquest. In 1204, King John 'Lackland' of England lost the Duchy to the French king, Philippe II, meaning that Normandy became divided into its mainland and insular territories. For the Channel Islands, France now became the enemy and, during the Hundred Years' War between England and France, Sark also experienced some conflict, with different groups of mercenaries and pirates seizing control. Indeed, over the centuries, the island's reputation as a base for pirates to lie in wait for unsuspecting ships to attack and plunder became so infamous that, in 1548, the French writer Rabelais described Sark and Herm in his work *Gargantua* as 'isles des forfans, des larrons, des briguans, des meurtriers et assassins' ('islands of pirates, thieves, scoundrels, murderers and assassins').

Sark was not permanently settled until 1565, when it was colonised by Hélier de Carteret, Seigneur of St. Ouen's parish in Jersey and his thirty-nine *tenants* (feudal landowners), who were granted a charter by Queen Elizabeth I. The decision to colonise came about as a consequence of the first French War of Religion (1562), when western

3

Jersey was felt to be vulnerable to attack from the French via Sark. De Carteret and his *tenants* would certainly have spoken Jersey's Norman tongue, Jèrriais, but the fact that Sark's little settlement was separated from Jersey by an often rough sea meant that communication was limited and, over the centuries, the speech of Jersey and Sark have diverged greatly, to the point that, today, speakers of Sercquiais and Jèrriais are unable to understand each other very well. Although Sark lies only six miles off the coast of Guernsey, Sercquiais is also markedly different from Guernésiais and from the now-extinct Norman language of Alderney, Auregnais.

When Victor Hugo visited Sark in 1859 for inspiration for his novel, *Les Travailleurs de la Mer* ('The Toilers of the Sea'), he was captivated by Sercquiais and went on to claim that 'Le paysan de Serk parle la langue de Louis XIV' ('The Sark peasant speaks the language of Louis XIV'). Indeed, according to some, the French word for octopus (*pieuvre*, used today as a synonym of *poulpe*), may actually be Sercquiais in origin. The word *pieuvre* was introduced by Hugo into the French language via this novel, in which one chapter describes a battle between a main character, Gilliatt, and one of the enormous octopuses inhabiting the waters around Sark.

Today, English is the usual everyday language of Sark. However, anglicisation occurred later than in the other Channel Islands and Sercquiais remained the main everyday language until well into the twentieth century. In 1787, one of John Wesley's missionaries who had been visiting Sark reported that, at that time, not a single family understood English. It seems likely that the presence of English stems from the arrival of English-speaking miners from Cornwall who, in the 1830s and 1840s, were brought to work in a lead-silver mine on Little Sark. The miners doubled Sark's then 250-strong population and, after the mines closed in 1847, many of the miners who left the island were accompanied by a Sark bride, which decreased further the number

4

of Sercquiais speakers. By the mid-nineteenth century, the wealthy English families who had established holiday residences in Sark were also contributing to the island's anglicisation, and this was increased further by the development of Sark's tourist industry in the latter half of the century, which brought regular visitors from England. By the end of the nineteenth century, the linguistic change was being commented on. For example, writing in the *Guernsey Magazine* of December 1875, the local historian Louisa Lane Clark observed 'the Sark patois is undergoing changes and gradually becoming extinct. The children do not now pronounce it so well ... nor with that seemly-careful and sharp sounding of every vowel and consonant, to be noticed in the speech of the older generation'.

The presence of English was strengthened further during the last twenty years of the nineteenth century, which brought an influx of immigrants to Sark, most of whom became permanent residents. In *The Fief of Sark*, Ewen and De Carteret describe this as having 'transformed the character of the island community [...] from a homogeneous group of people born in the island into a diverse assemblage with a steadily shrinking proportion of island-born inhabitants'. The local population was further diluted in the years following the First World War, when high taxes in the United Kingdom brought another wave of immigration to Sark and which led to many island families selling their properties (and even some *tenements* (land tenures)) to wealthy immigrants. By the 1930s, English had been adopted as the language of Sark's legislative assembly, *lê Chér Plê* (the Chief Pleas), and had replaced French as the official language of education and religion.

As only 129 of the then 600-strong population left Sark during the German Occupation, the Second World War probably had less of an anglicising influence on Sark than on the other Channel Islands. Despite the immigration that had occurred, at the end of the War Sark's population was still predominantly Norman-speaking and, in

1955, the Sark correspondent of the *Jersey Evening Post* wrote that twenty-one out of the island's thirty-six *tenants* were more fluent in Sercquiais than in English. However, during the second half of the century, the combination of migration and increased tourism began to take their linguistic toll. As early as 1960, only half the population of Sark had been born in the island and, in 1967, 61% of the dwellings were in the hands of non-islanders. At the end of the twentieth century, it was estimated that fewer than twenty of the then 610 permanent inhabitants of Sark (3.5%) spoke Sercquiais. The language ceased being passed down from one generation to the next several decades ago and, at the time of publication, only four native speakers of Sercquiais remain, all now elderly.

When any language dies, a community's culture and whole way of seeing the world are lost. As part of the attempt to keep Sercquiais alive, Sark's children have, since 2019, been learning the language of their ancestors at the Sark School. And yet, a language is more than its grammar – it also conveys a community's spirit. Proverbs and sayings, passed down through the generations, form part of the local culture and are generally well known because of their popular use in colloquial language. By using figurative language to make a statement about life, expressing a belief that is generally thought to be true, they represent a way for a community to transmit its common wisdom through the generations. With its declining number of speakers, many proverbs and sayings of Sercquiais have already been lost. Our aim has therefore been to set down those we still have so that these traditional and idiomatic expressions of the shared values of the Sercquiais community can be preserved for the future. Similar 'universal truths' may be found in many languages – indeed, given Sark's geographical location and linguistic situation, you will not be surprised to learn that some of the sayings contained in these pages have close counterparts in other Norman languages of the Channel Islands and, occasionally, in French and English. However, we have found that, even when the sayings match equivalents in these other languages, the exact formulation often bears a distinctive Sercquiais character.

Given the lack of opportunity to speak Sercquiais, no more than a small handful of the proverbs and sayings in this book are still recalled by the remaining native speakers. Most (and also a few Sercquiais riddles) would probably have been lost for all time had they not been written down by the Guernsey linguist John Peter Collas, Professor of French at Queen Mary College, London who, between the mid-1930s and mid-1950s, compiled a large collection of Channel Island words and expressions (including many hundreds of Sercquiais terms and sayings). Although Collas did not publish this material himself, it has now been fully edited and is published as *A Glossary of the Norman Language in the Channel Islands*. To Collas's remarkable list, we have added a few others: three from native speakers, two from the *Atlas linguistique et ethnographique normand* and one from the writings of the seventeenth-century Sark minister, Élie Brévint. In the interests of ensuring authenticity, all the sayings and riddles have been checked with the remaining native speakers.

So that the sayings can be accessible to the broadest possible audience, they are first provided in (idiomatic, rather than literal) English translation. These are accompanied by the original Sercquiais, both in transliteration (using the SNLC spelling system (Neudörfl 2022) which, at the time of publication, is the most comprehensively worked-out orthography for Sercquiais) and in the International Phonetic Alphabet (IPA). As with all languages, the pronunciation of different speakers of Sercquiais can vary. The pronunciation transcribed here represents that which is the most broadly acceptable.

We end by acknowledging all those who have contributed to this project. Our particular gratitude is expressed to Professor Jon Parry, of the University of Cambridge, for suggesting the project in the first instance, to the native speakers of Sercquiais for their expertise, their time and their good-will, and to the Priaulx Library, Guernsey and the Collas family for allowing us access to the material collected by John Peter Collas. The warm support received from Steve Foote, at Blue Ormer, for agreeing to publish the book and from Martin Remphry, whose superb illustrations help make the sayings and riddles come alive, is deeply appreciated. We are also delighted that Blue Ormer are publishing some of the sayings, with their Remphry illustrations, as a series of greeting cards. Finally, we wish to thank the institutions that have funded our work: respectively, the University of Cambridge and the Société Sercquaise/Charles University, Prague (Project UK No. 816218).

We hope you enjoy the Sark sayings!

To learn more about the language of Sark visit the website www.bonjhur.net.

Mari C. Jones (Professor of French Linguistics and Language
    Change, University of Cambridge)
Martin Neudörfl (Charles University, Prague), July 2022.

References

Brasseur, Patrice 1980, 1984, 1997, 2010. *Atlas linguistique et ethnographique normand*. Paris: CNRS, (2010: Caen: Presses Universitaires de Caen).

Ewen, Alfred H. and Allan R. De Carteret 1969. *The Fief of Sark*. Guernsey: The Guernsey Press Co. Ltd.

Jones, Mari C. 2022. *A Glossary of the Norman Language in the Channel Islands*. Guernsey: Blue Ormer.

Neudörfl, Martin 2022. *Sark Norman Language Codification* (SNLC). Prague: Charles University.

WEATHER

Beware a mild April.
Avrił l'dů, ch'ê l'pîre d'tů.
[ävrɪ lə dʊ:ə̯ ʃ ɛ: lə pɪ:ər də tʊ:ə̯]

We'll have good weather tomorrow because the dor-beetles are grumbling.
J'éron byòtân dṃen kar lz'êčérbô rondre.
[d͡ʒ ɛrɔ̃y̯ bjɔ:tã: dmɛ̃ kär ləz ɛ:cɛrbɔy̯ rɔ̃y̯ndr]

Rain in February is worth a good pile of dung.
(rain in February is highly valued in Sark)
La płì du Mê d'Févry vò un vyaje d'conrě.
[lä pʎɪ:ə̯ dy mwɛ: d fɛvrɪ vɔ: ỹ: vjɑd͡ʒ d kɔ̃y̯reə̯]

Rain in March isn't worth a gannet's droppings.
(rain in March is not highly valued in Sark)
La płì d'Mar ne vò pâ une mérde d'gar.
[lä pʎɪ:ə̯ d mär nə vɔ: pɑ: ỹn mɛrd d gär]

A mackerel sky and a made-up woman are both forms of beauty that do not last for long.
Syełe gavlé, filye fardè, sôn dê byòtè ben vite pâsè.
[sjəʎ gävlɛ fɪʎj färdɛ: sɔ̃y̯ de: bjɔ:tɛ: bɛ̃ vɪt pɑ:sɛ:]

9

Rain before Christmas makes the springs rise, if they don't rise before Christmas, they won't stay afterwards.

Lê plî ḍvàn Nuĕł fôn lê ṛṡůrṡe montĕ, si i'n bŭje pâ ḍvàn Nuĕł, i'n monte pâ aprê půr tnin.

[le: pʌɪːə̞ dvã: nwɛ fɔ̃ʊ: le: rsʊrs mɔ̃ʊ̞ʈe̞ə̞, s ɪ n bʊ̞d͡ʒ pɑ: dvã: nwɛ, ɪ n mɔ̃ʊ̞ʈ pɑ: äprɛ: pʊr tnẽɪ̞]

A rainbow in the West: good weather in the West.

Arkansyél an Vuè: byòtân půr Vuè.

[ärkɑ̃:sjɛl ã: vwɛ: bjɔ:tã: pʊr vwɛ:]

When the sun sets red in the evening, it's a sign of good weather to come, when the sun is red as it rises in the morning, it's a sign of bad weather.

Kàn l'soléł s'cŭche rŭje, ch'ê l'siṅe d'byòtân, kàn l'soléł s'lĕve rŭje, ch'ê l'siṅe d'mòvê tân.

[kã: l sɔʊ̞lɛ s kʊ̞ə̞ʃ rʊ̞ə̞d͡ʒ, ʃ ɛ: l sẽɪ̞n d bjɔ:tã: kã: l sɔʊ̞lɛ s lɛɪ̞v rʊ̞ə̞d͡ʒ ʃ ɛ: l sẽɪ̞n d mɔ:ʊ̞vʷɛ: tã:]

When you see the heron, tie down your house, because it's a sign of bad weather.

Kàn tu vê l'héran, amare ta mĕzon, kar ch'ê l'siṅe d'mòvê tân.

[kã: tɣ vʷɛ: l hɛrã ämä:r tä mwɛ:zɔ̃ʊ̞, kar ʃ ɛ: l sẽɪ̞n d mɔ:ʊ̞vʷɛ: tã:]

10

A rainbow in the West: good weather in the West.

We'll have fine weather tomorrow because the bats are out flying.

We'll have fine weather tomorrow because the bats are out flying.

J'éron byòtân dṃen kar lê cotsụ̆rî vole.

[d͡ʒ ɛrɔ̃y̨ bjɔːtɑ̃: dm̥ɛ̃ kar lɛː kɔy̨tsʊɔrɪːʒ̈ vɔy̨l]

A mackerel sky means rain in twenty-four hours.

Syełe calyboté, d'la pł̀ì dân vínkatře eure.

[sjəʎ kaʎbɔʊtɛ d lä pʎɪːʒ̈ dɑ̃: vɪnkatr œːɣr]

Geese in the distance means a storm is near, geese nearby is a sign of good weather.

Pîrô d'łen, ğêle d'prê, pîrô d'prê, ch'ê l'siṅe d'byòtân.

[pɪjɛraːy̨ də ʎɛ ɟɛːl də praːɹ pɪjɛraːy̨ də praːɹ ʃ ɛː l sɛ̃n̪ də bjɔːtɑ̃:]

If the claws of the moon point upwards, it's a sign of bad weather.

Si la leune a lê grîn an hòt, ch'ê l'siṅe d'grôtân.

[sɪ lä lœɣn ä lɛː grɛ̃: ɑ̃: hɔː ʃ ɛː l sɛ̃n̪ d grɔy̨tɑ̃:]

THE FARM

You shouldn't prepare the stall before the calf has arrived.

I'n fò pâ trimĕ l'êtablye ḍvàn ke l'vyò n'vènje.

[ɪ n fɔ: pɑ: trɪmwɛ l ɛ:tabʌj dvã: kə lə vjɔ: n vẽ:d͡ʒ]

It's a sad state of affairs when the hen clucks before the cockerel crows.

(used to describe when a girl takes the initiative in affairs of the heart)

Ch'ê tristre kàn la půle chante ḍvàn l'cok.

[ʃ ɛ: trɪstr kã: lä pʊl ʃã:t dvã: l kɔʊ̯k]

He's as fussy as a hen who only has one chick.

Il'ê ambarasé cůme une půle ki n'a k'un pǔchin.

[ɪl ɛ: ã:bäräsɛ kʊm ỹn pʊl kɪ n ä k ỹ: pwɔʃễ]

You could go to the well ninety-nine times but the hundredth time you could still fall in.

Tu pǔřê alĕ á la fonténe nenante neuf fê mê la chăntìme fê tu pǔřê čê ḍdân.

[tʏ pwɛrɛ: älɐ̝ ä lä fɔ̃ʏ̯tɛn nənã:t nœf fɑ:ɪ mwɛ: lä ʃãtɪ:ə̝m fwɛ: tʏ pwɛrɛ: cɛ: d:ã:]

You could go to the well ninety-nine times...

A woman who grumbles and a hen who is laying make noise in the house.

Fame ki grôn é pǔle ki pôn fét du brit
dân la mězon.

[fãm kɪ grɔ̃ʊ̯ pʊl kɪ pɔ̃ʊ̯ fɛ dɤ brɪt dã: lä mwɛ:zɔ̃ʊ̯]

She's got no more character than a sow that eats her piglets.

(a very grave insult as, in Sark, a sow is well known as a caring mother)

Ǔ'n a pâ pû d'naturéle k'une trì ki manje
sê (ptî) cǔchôn.

[ʊ n ä pɑ: pɤ: d nätɤrɛl k ỹn trɪ:ə̯ kɪ mã:d͡ʒ sɛ: (ptɪ:) kwɔʃã:ʊ̯]

There's enough for all the Tostevins.

(i.e. there's plenty on the table for all of us.
The Tostevins are a large Guernsey family).

I'y an a asè pǔr tǔ lê Tôtvîn.

[ɪ j (ãn) ä äsɛ: pʊr tʊ:ə̯ lɛ: tɔʊ̯tvẽ:]

INSECTS

You won't catch a fly with salt.

Ch'ê pâ atůt du séł ke nǫ̌'hape dê moke.

[ʃ ɛ: pɑ: ätʊ dɤ sɛ kə nʊ:ǫ̌ hɑp dɛ: mɔɣk]

Even flies and gnats want to know how they're made.

I'n y a pâ d'moke ni bibét ki n'veulye savě
cůme il'ê fět.

[ɪ nʲ j ä pɑ: nɪ mɔʊk nɪ bɪbɛt ki n vœʎ sävʷɛ kʊm ɪl
ɛ: fwɛt]

There's enough for all the Tostevins.

17

ANIMALS

He hasn't yet seen the beast that'll eat him.

(i.e. he still has a lot to learn)

I'n a pâ veu la bête ki s'an va l'manjĭ.

[ɪ n ä pɑ: vœ᷈ə lä bwɛ:t kɪ s ã: va l mã:d͡ʒɪ]

**A horse that hasn't eaten oats isn't going
to be very quick.**

Un jhva ki n'a (pâ) jhamê manjĭ d'avéne ne s'an va
pâ avĕ grânt'yère.

[ỹ: ʒvä k ɪ n ä (pɑ:) ʒ̃ãmwɛ: mã:d͡ʒɪ d'även nə s ã:
vä pɑ: ävʷə᷈ə grã:tʲ jɛ:r]

We don't speak about a fox without seeing its tail.

(i.e. talk of the Devil!)

J'n pâlon pâ d'un řnard sân k'tu vê sa cừ.

[d͡ʒə n pɑːlɔ̃ỵ pɑː d ỹː (r)när sɑ̃ː k tɤ vʷɛː sä kʊːạ]

A good sheaf of oats will do him more good than a lash of a whip.

(said to a man who whips a horse)

Une bůne ğérbe d'avéne li vò mû k'une lache de fuét.

[ỹn bwɔ̃n ɟɛrb d ävɛn lɪ vɔː mɤː k ỹn laʃ d fwɛt]

A horse that hasn't eaten oats isn't going to be very quick.

You can't make a donkey drink if it isn't thirsty.

Nᵾ'n peut pâ fĕre bĕre une âne si ᵾ'n a pâ d'séu.

[nʊː n pœ(ɣ) pɑː fwɛːr bwɛːr ỹn ɑ̃ːn sɪ ʊ n ä pɑː d sɛɣ̞]

A dog will go a lot less further without the blast of a whistle.

(used to describe people who are too proud to ask for help)

Un čhan va ben ptit k'i n'va pâ ò sûfłét.

[ỹː t͡ʃɒ̃ kɪ vä bẽ ptɪt k ɪ n vä pɑː ɔɣ̞ sʏːfʌɛt]

You can't make a donkey drink if it isn't thirsty.

What has never been and never will be – a mouse's nest in a cat's ear.

What has never been and never will be – a mouse's nest in a cat's ear.

Či ki n'a jhamê té, é jhamê n'ṣsa – un nik de sŭrì dân l'ŭřélye d'un cat.

[cɪ kɪ n ä ʒãmwɛ: tɛ ɛ ʒãmwɛ: n s:ä] – [ỹ: nɪk d suɔrɪ: dã: l wɛrɛʎj d ỹ: kɑt]

BIRDS

**Birds of the same feather gather together
on the same bank.**

Lz'uézyò du mème płumaje luz'asamblye
sû l'mème rivaje.

[ləz wɛ:zjɔ: dɣ mɛ:m pʌɣmad͡ʒ lɣ:z äsã:bʌjə sɣ:
l mɛ:m rɪvad͡ʒ]

A bird in a cage is worth two in the branches.

Un uézĕ an caje, vò deû dân lê branke.

[ỹ(:)n wɛ:zɐ̞ ã: kad͡ʒ vɔ: dœ: dã: lɛ: brã:k]

A bird in a cage is worth two in the gorsebush.

Un uézĕ dân une caje, vò deû dân une jŭñìre.

[ỹn wɛ:zɐ̞ dã: ỹn kad͡ʒ vɔ: dœ: dã: ỹn d͡ʒʊɲɪ:r]

Crows and pigeons don't perch together.

Lê cŏrbîn é lê pijôn n'juke pâ ansamblye.

[lɛ: kɣrbẽ: ɛ lɛ: pɪd͡ʒɔ̃ṳ n d͡ʒɣk pa: ã:sã:bʌj]

The Meaning of Life

Beauty without goodness is nothing but vanity.
Byòté sân bonté n'ê ke vanité.
[bjɔ:tɛ sã: bɔ̃ɡ̊tɛ n ɛ: kə vänɪtɛ]

He who only listens to one bell only hears one sound.
(i.e. listen to both sides)
Le ṡyen ki'n wét k'une cłoche n'wét k'un son.
[l sjɛ̃ kɪ nə wɛ k ỹn kʌɔ̊ʃ nə wɛ k ỹ: sɔ̃ɡ̊]

A good reputation is worth more than a golden belt.
Bůne renůmè vò mû k'une chènture důrè.
[bwɔ̃n rənʊmɛ: vɔ: mʏ: k ʏn ʃɛ̃:tʏ:r dʊɡ̊rɛ:]

He's too big for his boots.
Il'ê tro grânt půr sê bote.
[ɪl ɛ: trɔɡ̊ grã: pʊr sɛ: bɔʊt]

**He who gives up before dying must be ready
to suffer greatly.**
Le ṡyen ki's důne hòt d̦vàn mů̦ri dět s'atandre
á ben sůfri.
[lə sjɛ̃ kɪ dʊn hɔ: dvã: mwɔrɪ dɛ(ɪ̦t) s ätã:dr ä bɛ̃
sʊfrɪ]

It's a long road that only has one destination.

Ch'ê une longe rù ki n'a ren k'un but.

[ʃ ɛ: ʏn lɔ̃ʊ̯gə rʏ: kɪ n ä rɛ̃ k ỹ: bʏt]

There's no smoke without fire.

I'n y a pâ d'fumè sân feuc.

[ɪ nʲ j ä pɑ: d fʏmɛ: sɑ̃: fœɤ̯k]

Don't put off until tomorrow what you can do today.

N'ṛmét pâ á ḍmen ṡyé'k tu peû fěre aňét.

[nə rmɛ pɑ: ä dmɛ̃ sjɛ k tʏ pœ: fwɛ:r ɑ̃ɲɛt]

Order lasts but disorder doesn't.

Bůne rěglye dure mê dêrěglye n dure pâ.

[bwɔ̃n rɛɪ̯gʎj dʏ:r mwɛ: dɛ:rɛɪ̯gʎj n dʏ:r pɑ:]

He who earns well and who spends a lot doesn't have much left at the end of the year.

L'ṡyen ki gâṅe dur é ki dêpanse hardi ò but dl'anè, n'vět pâ grânt choze.

[l sjɛ̃ kɪ gɑ̃:n dʏr ɛ dɛ:pɑ̃:s härdɪ ɔ:ʊ̯ bʏt d l ɑ̃nɛ:
n vʷɛ pɑ: grɑ̃: ʃɔʊ̯z]

The late man never calls the early one.

(i.e. it's better to be early).

Jhamê le ṡyen k'ê tard ne crî ò ṡyen k'ê heure.

[ʒɑ̃mwɛ: l sjɛ̃ k ɛ: tär nə krɪ:ə ɔ:ʊ̯ sjɛ̃ k ɛ: hœ:r]

It's a long road that only has one destination.

(A good liar) steers close to the truth without actually touching it.

Chtinna n'ê pâ sǔvant łen d'la věrité sân y tǔchǐ.

[ʃt(ẽ)ᵢn:ä n ɛ: pɑ: sʊvã ʎẽ d lä vʷɛritɛ sã: ɪ tʊʃɪ]

Service of the good and the great is no benefice.

Sérvise d'mǔsyeuř n'ê pâ éritaje.

(today, the term *mǔsyeuř* means 'tourists')

[sɛrvɪs d mʊsjœr n ɛ: pɑ: ɛrɪtad͡ʒ]

The wind is never at the poor man's door because the poor man never has any shelter.

Le věnt n'ê pâ tréjǔř dân l'û du pǔre ǔme, kar jhamê i'n ṣsět á l'abritre.

[lə vãt n ɛ: pɑ: tred͡ʒʊ:ǫ dã: l ɤ: dɤ pʊǫr ɔǫm kar ʒãmwɛ: n s:ɛt ä l äbrɪtr]

Great wind: no shelter – poor man: no friend. When he has a beautiful wife, you take her and kiss her and the poor man is never happy.

Grô věnt: pâ d'abritre - pǔre ǔme: pâ d'ami. Kàn il'a une běle fame, tu li prân é li běze, é l'pǔre ǔme n'ê jhamê á sn'éze.

[grɔǫ vãt pɑ: d äbrɪtr pʊǫr ɔǫm pɑ: d ämɪ kã: ɪl ä ỹn bwɛl fãm, tɤ lɪ prã: ɛ tɤ lɪ bwɛ:z ɛ l pʊǫr ɔǫm n ɛ: ʒãmwɛ: ä sn ɛ:z]

He who knows all that can be known is a god among men; he who knows all that he should know is a man among beasts; he who only knows what he should know is a beast among men.

L'śyen ki sĕt tŭt śyé'ki s'peut savĕ ê dyeu ăntre lz'ŭme; l'śyen ki sĕt tŭt śyé'k i'dĕt savĕ ê ŭme ăntre lê bête; l'śyen ki n'sĕt ke śyé'k i'dĕt savĕ ê bête ăntre lz'ŭme.

[lə sjɛ̃ kɪ sɛ tʊ(t) sjɛ kɪ s pœ(ɣt) sävʷɐ̹ ɛ: ɖʲjœ ɑ̃tr ləz (ɔ̃)ʊ̹m lə sjɛ̃ ki sɛ tʊ(t) sjɛ k ɪ dɛ(ɪ̞t) sävʷɐ̹ ɛ: ɔ̃ʊ̹m ɑ̃tr lɛ: bwɛ:t l sjɛ̃ kɪ n sɛ k sjɛ k ɪ dɛ(ɪ̞t) sävʷɐ̹ ɛ: bwɛ:t ɑ̃tr ləz (ɔ̃)ʊ̹m]

Youth fades like a flower.

La jónèse pâse cŭme une fłeŭr.

[lä jɔ̃nɛ:s pɑ:s kʊm ɤn fʎœ(ɣ/r)]

Youth fades like a flower.

27

THE SEA

What comes with the flow returns with the ebb.
Ṡyé'ki vĕnt d'flot s'an ṛvenra d'ébe.
[sjɛ kɪ vẽt d fʌɔɣt s ã: rvẽrä d ɛb]

**You're unlikely to light your pipe in
thirty fathoms of water.**
Tu n'ê pa seuř d'alumĕ ta pipe á trănte brache d'yò.
[tɤ n ɛ: pɑ: sœ: älɣmweˌ tä pɪp ä trãt braʃ dʲ jɔ:]

Where there's a big hole, you'll need a big plank.

MAKING THINGS

Even a good worker will have his faults.

I'n y a pâ si bûn ůvry ki n'ê san fòt.

[ɪ n j ä pɑ: sɪ bwũn ʊvrɪ kɪ n ɛ: sã: fɔ:]

Don't use two nails where you only need one.

Ne mét pâ deû cl̥ů lá, y ů k'i n'an fò k'yeun.

[nə mɛ pɑ: dœ: kʌʊ: lä j ʊ k ɪ n ã: fɔ: k jœ̃]

Where there's a big hole, you'll need a big plank.

Lá, ů ê k'i y a un grânt creû, i'fò une grânt pl̥anche.

[lä w ɛ k ɪ j ä ỹ: grã: krœ: ɪ fɔ: ỹn grã: pʌã:ʃ]

THE BODY

I prefer seeing his heels to his toes.

J'éme mû vê sê talôn ke sê bû d'pî.

[d͡ʒ ɛm mʏ: vʷɛ: sɛ: tälɔ̃ʊ̯ kə sɛ: bʏ: d pɪ:ə̯]

He's just made a promise with his tongue that he won't be able to undo with his teeth.

(said when wedding bells are heard or to a man who has just got married)

Nevlá yeun ki vent d'fĕre une promêse důve sa lange k'i n'ŗdêftha pâ důve sê dân.

[nɛvlä jœ̃ kɪ vɛt də fwɛ:r ỹn prɔmwɛ:s dʊv sä lã:g k ɪ n rdɛ:fcä pɑ: dʊv sɛ: dã:]

He has a short neck! He'll be hanged.

(i.e. he looks like a brute, he will be hanged)

Il'ê cůrt d'co! I'ṣsa pandu.

[ɪl ɛ: kʊr də kɔʊ̯ ɪ s:ä pɔ̃:dʏ]

Don't spit too high or it'll fall back into your mouth.

(i.e. don't be too confident)

I'n fò pâ bavĕ tro hòt, ů ben ů vû ŗčêra dân la bůche.

[ɪ n fɔ: pɑ: bavʷɛ trɔʊ̯ hɔ: ʊ bɛ̃ ʊ vʊ:ə̯ rcɛ:rä dã: lä bʊə̯ʃ]

Don't spit into a strong wind or it'll fall back into your mouth

(i.e. don't be too ambitious)

I'n fò pâ bavĕ dân un grânt vănt ů ben i't ṛčêra dân la bǔche.

[ɪ n fɔ: pɑ: bavʷɛ dɑ̃: ỹ: grɑ̃: vɑ̃t ʊ bɛ̃ ɪ tə rcɛ:rä dɑ̃: lä bʊə̥ʃ]

I prefer seeing his heels to his toes.

THE NATURAL WORLD

As soon as the sun is up, the seeds should be put out to dry.
Òsivite ke l'soléł s'lĕve, i'fò métre la gréne á sči.
[ɔ:ʊ̯sɪvɪt k l sɔʊ̯lɛ s leɪ̯v ɪ fɔ: mɛtr lä grɛn ä scɪ]

Cut your willow in January and February because in March it'll be too late.
Janvy, Févry, cope tan ozy, kar dân l'Mê d'Mar, il'ê tro tard.
[d͡ʒɑ̃:vɪ fɛvrɪ kɔʊ̯p tɑ̃:n ɔʊ̯zɪ kär dɑ̃: lə mwɛ: d mär ɪ l ɛ: trɔʊ̯ tär]

In the Spring all is good but in September nothing is the same.
Ò Ṛnůvĕ tůt ê bĕ mê dân l'mê d'Séptambre ren n'ṛsamblye.
[ɔ:ʊ̯ rnʊvɐ̯ tʊt ɛ: bwɐ̯ mwɛ: dɑ̃: l mwɛ: d sɛptɑ̃:br rɛ̃ nə rsɑ̃:bʌ(j)]

DAYS OF THE WEEK

Saturday's fine-ness doesn't last till Monday.
La byòté du Sámdi n'dure pâ jusk'ò Leûndi.
[lä bjɔ:tɛ dʏ sãmdɪ n dʏ:r pɑ: jʏsk ɔ:ʊ̯ lœ̃:ɣ̞dɪ]

**Once Sunday's dripped away, the week
will soon follow.**
Kàn l'dîmanche ḏgǔte, la sṃéne s'an bĕtô suîra.
[kã: l dẽ̞mã:ʃ dgʊt lä smɛn s ã: swɪjɛra]

Once Sunday's dripped away, the week will soon follow.

RIDDLES

Question: **What looks most like a tomcat sitting on its hind quarters?**

Či ki ŗsamblye l'pû á un cat asî sû san ḍrìre?

[cɪ kɪ rsɑ̃:bʌj l pɣ: ä ỹ: kɑt äsɪ: sɣ: sɑ̃: drɪ:r]

Answer: **A female cat.**

Une cate.

[ỹn kɑt]

Question: **What is long, very long and has pegs all along it?**

Či k'ê lông, ben lông, é gvilye tůt'l tůt?

[cɪ k ɑ: lɔ̃ʏ̯ bɛ lɔ̃ʊ ɛ gviʎ tʊ l tʊt]

Answer: **A bramble.**

Une ronche.

[ʏn rɔ̃ʏ̯ʃ]

What looks most like a tomcat sitting on its hind quarters?

What goes on the water and under the water but never touches the water?

Question: **What goes on the water and under
the water but never touches the water?**

Či ki va sû l'yò è sŭ l'yò é jhamê n'tǔche pâ á l'yò?

[cɪ kɪ vä sʏ: ʎ jɔ: ɛ sʊ: э̧ ʎ jɔ: ɛ ӡɑ̃mwɛ: n tʊʃ ä ʎ jɔ:]

Answer: **A duck's egg.**

Un euf d'une canote.

[ỹn œf d ỹn kɑ̃nɔʊ̧t]

Question: **What goes all around the field and
stops at the gate?**

Či ki fét tǔt l'tǔt du cłô é s'arête á la hěche?

[cɪ ki fɛ tʊ l tʊt dʏ kʎɑ:ʊ̧ ɛ s ärɛ:t ä la hɛɪʃ]

Answer: **The hedge.**

Le fôsét.

[lə fɔʊ̧sɛt]

Question: **Put shaggy against shaggy and the
poor naked spot is covered. What am I?**

Mét plu contre plu é cǔvre l'povre nu. Ci'k ch'ê?

[mɛ plʏ kɔ̃ʊ̧tr plʏ é kʊvr l pɔʊ̧vr nʏ] [cɪ k ʃ ɑ:ị]

Answer: **An eye.**

Un yi.

[ỹɲ ɪ]

ILLUSTRATOR'S NOTE

I was delighted when Steve Foote asked me to illustrate *Sark Sayings*. Growing up on Sark I would listen to my grandmother speaking Sark Patois as she called it, often reverting to Sercquiais when she wanted to talk about something not meant for my ears (understandably I picked up a number of swear words).

I have tried to include many of the island's beauty spots such as the Window in the Rock, La Coupée and Creux Harbour as well as some Sark traditions, the Good Friday sailing of toy boats on Beauregard Pond and a Sark Dinner of boiled pork and rouleux, a giant currant dumpling wrapped in a cabbage leaf and steamed on top of the meat. The Cat Rock was an apt scene for the cat riddle and no horse could set off from the Collinette without its oats. My apologies to Olympic Gold winner Carl Hester for depicting him on Jacko, the donkey he learnt to ride whilst on Sark.

As mentioned in the earlier introduction it was the arrival of the Cornish miners which participated the eventual decline of the Sark language. Amongst their number were three Remphry brothers, one of who remained on the island, my many-times great grandfather. Thanks to the work of both Mari C. Jones and Martin Neudörfl Sercquiais will not be lost forever.

Martin Remphry
July 2022